'THE QUEEN OF WATERING PLACES'

Loved and celebrated since her Regency heyday, which culminated in the completion of the Royal Pavilion for the new king, George IV, the town of Brighton remains one of Britain's most popular and enduring resorts. From the sea, both Brighton and the adjacent town of Hove present an elegant facade of great crescents, sweeping terraces and open squares for some three miles along the shore, testament to the rapid development of the late eighteenth and early nineteenth centuries.

The origins of these two towns are much older, as significant finds from the Neolithic age onwards indicate. The settlement was well established by the time William the Conqueror took his great census of the country in 1086 in the Domesday book. By the late sixteenth century Brighton was the largest town in Sussex. In 1580 the government of the town was regulated by 'The Booke of Ancient Customs of Brighthelmston'. This ensured, amongst other things, the maintenance of the town's defences.

Such actions as were taken, however, could do nothing to protect the town against the elements, or her inhabitants against growing competition. The sea crept steadily further inland, eventually destroying the lower town completely in 1705 after a great storm. Having lost their homes, the fishermen began to loose their livelihoods. But the sea was to give Brighton another chance. In 1750, a local doctor, practising at Lewes, published a treatise advocating the revitalising properties of sea-water bathing and drinking. He sent his patients to Brighton, and within a

speculation about their relationship. (She was actually only thirty at the time).

Below: **Mermaids at Brighton**, by W.Heath, 1829. Visitors are shown indulging in the healthy pleasures of sea bathing.

Below left: **Morning Promenade upon the Cliffs, Brighton**
Anonymous
Published January 1806
Brighton society is shown donkey riding, divided into the 'Active Sett', 'Kicking Sett' and 'Passive Sett'.

The West Front, Royal Pavilion, Brighton
Aquantint by John Nash, 1826.

short space of time, a healthy holiday by the sea was to become a British institution. The seaside resort was born, and Brighton never looked back.

From the 1760's, amusements and diversions were introduced for the visiting holiday makers, with the opening of Assembly Rooms, theatres and libraries and the laying out of walks for promenading. Brighton was swiftly becoming the place for fashionable society to congregate, and in 1783 the young Prince of Wales joined them.

After the austerity and stuffiness of his father's court at Windsor, Prince George quickly succumbed to the glamour of Brighton. He returned frequently, and after secretly marrying Maria Fitzherbert in 1785, decided to take a permanent home in the town, purchasing a modest farmhouse in 1786. Brighton House, as it was known, would over the coming decades be transformed into the extraordinary palace which dominates the town today - the Royal Pavilion.

As King George IV, he did not live long to enjoy the completed building, and upon his death in 1830, the palace passed to his successor, William IV, but neither the town nor the palace were much to the taste of his successor, Queen Victoria, and Brighton's Royal patronage ended in 1845.

The retirement of the monarch did nothing to diminish the popularity of 'Doctor Brighton', however. The railway brought the crowds from London in increasing numbers, and by the end of the nineteenth century the West and Palace piers were built, and the growing town of Hove became a popular residence for wealthy retirees.

Brighton and Hove today have effectively become a single great town, indeed they hope together to be granted city status in time for the next century, ensuring the future of 'The Queen of Watering Places' for generations to come.

THE SEAFRONT

A stroll along the seafront on a warm summer's evening is one of the pleasures of Brighton. In fact it's best to start in Hove, from the seafront lawns opposite Adelaide Crescent *(photograph right)*. Here rows of old-fashioned wooden beachhuts lead up to the border between the two towns, marked by a peace memorial known locally as 'The Angel' *(photograph bottom right)*. The statue stands almost opposite Brunswick Square *(photograph below)*, part of the Brunswick Town development of 1824. This estate was intended to be quite self contained, and was managed under the governance of an Act of Parliament from 1830. It had its own Town Hall, and the administration was to eventually cover all of the growing town of Hove. The original regulations governing the painting of houses still stand, and all properties in the area wear the same creamy livery, which must be repainted every three years, enabling the estate to retain it's character today.

A little further along the seafront is the derelict West Pier, built in 1863 for the growing western side of the town. Closed for over twenty years and badly decayed, it still has a ghostly elegance in the morning mists. It is now owned by a trust which plans to restore it to Victorian splendour.

Just beyond the Pier, one reaches Brighton's two most splendid hotels, the Metropole and the Grand. The Metropole was designed by Alfred Waterhouse, the Victorian architect probably best known for the Natural

History Museum in London, and Manchester Town Hall.

The nearby Grand is some thirty years older, recently completely restored after the notorious bombing on October 12th 1984, when IRA terrorists attempted the assassination of the Prime Minister and Cabinet, resident in the hotel during their annual party conference. The hotel was built in the Italian style by the architect John Whichcord.

Further along, past the modern Brighton Centre, is the Old Ship Hotel, the oldest in the town. Although the seafront is nineteenth century, the core of the building is older, and the Ship Inn was trading in 1665. Below it on the beach is Brighton's Fishing Museum, close to the site of the former fish market in the King's Road Arches. The museum records the rise and fall of the fisheries, and includes a 'hoggie', the broad vessel suited to the local waters. Although the industry has all but died in the town, an annual Mackerel Fair still celebrates the first landing of the season, and from time to time shoals of mackerel can still be seen roiling the waters close to the shore.

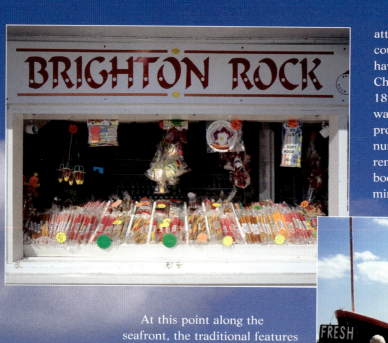

attraction, and one of the finest in the country. It was first opened in 1899, having been built to replace the former Chain Pier, destroyed by a storm in 1896. The present Pier's oriental design was no doubt influenced by its proximity to the Royal Pavilion, and a number of the original features still remain, such as the fishscale-roofed booths, filigree wrought iron arches and minaret kiosks. The Palace Pier offers all

At this point along the seafront, the traditional features of the British seaside begin to crowd in; amusement halls, fish and chip shops, cafes and crazy golf, culminating in the famous Palace Pier. This is probably Brighton's most popular

The interior retains an impressive hall decorated with fine marble carving.

Close by, Volk's Railway *(photograph left)* runs for a little over a mile from Madeira Drive to the Marina. It was built by Magnus Volk, a local inventor, and was the first public electric railway in the country. When first opened in 1883, the track covered just 300 yards, but the novelty of the ride ensured the success of a 'sea voyage on wheels', and the line was gradually expanded over the years.

the traditional amusements of the seaside: Brighton Rock, candyfloss, whelk stalls, palmists and a funfair. At night it is elaborately illuminated *(photograph inside front cover)*.

Opposite the Palace Pier on the corner of Madeira Drive stands the Brighton Aquarium, built in 1872 in the italianate style, and still used as a display centre for marine wildlife *(photograph right)*.

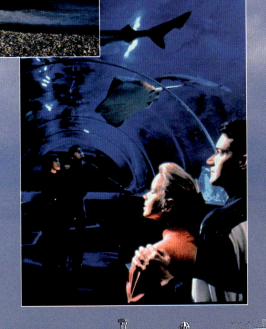

Just above, on Marine Parade, the Royal Escape pub commemorates another of the town's Royal connections. It was from Brighton that King Charles IV escaped to France after his defeat at Worcester. On the morning of the fifteenth of October 1651, he sailed in a coal boat to Fecamp in France, not to return until the Restoration nine years later. His flight is re-enacted every year in an annual race.

Madeira Drive runs alongside the massive sea-wall of the East Cliff, connected to the terrace above by an elegant lift, housed in an oriental style kiosk decorated with mythical animals. From here the wide esplanade of Marine Parade runs past the Royal Crescent *(photograph below)*, distinguished from the majority of Brighton's sea-front architecture by its cladding of black mathematical tiles. This was the first residential development built facing the sea. The developer attempted to curry favour by erecting a large statue of the Prince Regent in front of the Crescent. Unfortunately, parts of it broke away quite quickly, and the Prince was not amused. The most famous resident of the Royal Crescent was the Shakespearian actor Lord Olivier of Brighton, who lived at number 4 for some twenty years.

The largest development on this side of Brighton is Kemp Town, at the extreme eastern end of Marine Parade, and the forerunner of the Brunswick estate at the start of this walk.

The estate opens with Chichester terrace, a group of seafront houses notable for their robust Doric porches which support conservatories above. Beyond is the magnificent Lewes Crescent *(photograph left)*, with Sussex Square behind it. Kemp Town has many famous former residents, including Princess Louise, daughter of Edward VII (1 Lewes Crescent), Lewis Carroll (11 Sussex Square) and Dame Anna Neagle (18 Lewes Crescent). The gardens of Lewes Crescent and Sussex Square are privately owned by the residents, but the Kemp Town slopes below are now public gardens.

THE OLD TOWN AND LANES

Brighton's famous Lanes, the shopping quarter most popular with visitors to the town, consists of a maze of narrow alleyways connecting the principal streets of the Old Town: Ship Street, Middle Street, Black Lion Street and East Street, bisected by Duke Street, Prince Albert Street and Bartholomews Although only a small area, the constant criss-crossing and sudden turns make it easy to loose your bearings. The best way to enjoy The Lanes is to drift through them and see what you find.

The earliest known map of Brighton, from around 1520, shows this area ablaze after an attack by the French. Most of the buildings were destroyed, and it is only the layout of streets that reflect the old town of Brighthelmstone, the buildings themselves being mostly eighteenth and nineteenth century.

Most visitors will start from East Street, opposite the India Gate entrance from the Royal Pavilion. The road runs to the seafront, but turn up the alley alongside the Sussex Tavern to reach Market Street and Brighton Place. The Pump House pub which dominates this little square has long been the site of an inn, and may take its name from the old town well which was nearby, or from the

traditional title of Pump Room, where spa, or in Brighton's case, sea water was drunk for health.

From this point, there are several routes into The Lanes. Facing the Pump House, the extreme right takes you through the modern Brighton Square, with its Dolphin Fountain, and on into Meeting House Lane. Said to be haunted by a grey nun, this narrow alley will lead you on past the Bath Arms into Union Street. The Greek style Chapel on the left, now a public house, is said to be where the explorer Dr Livingstone was married in 1844.

Turning left from the Pump House will bring you to Bartholemews, and the imposing classical facade of the Town Hall *(photograph below)*, built in 1830. Beyond it is the modern civic square, and tourist information centre. The road continues through Prince Albert Street, to reach Ship Street, the principal thoroughfare in the Lanes area. From here, any turning or alleyway will lead you on into the heart of old Brighton.

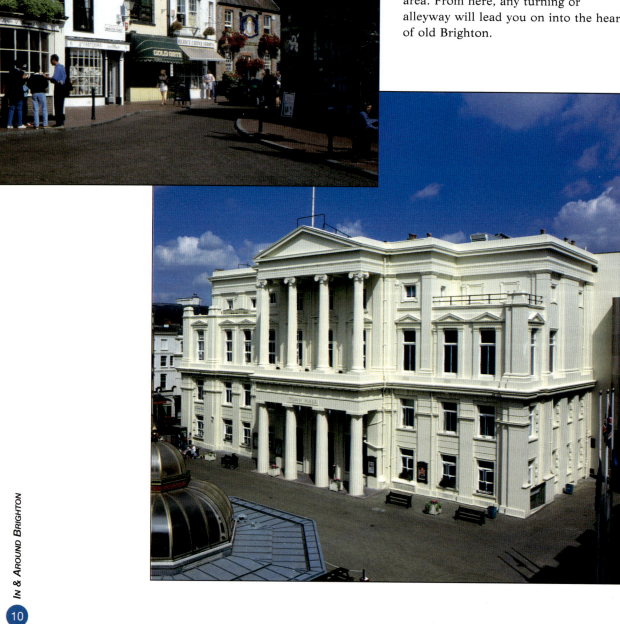

OLD STEINE AND NORTH LAINE

The wide promenade running northwards from the sea alongside the Royal Pavilion *(photograph above)* is the Old Steine, originally used by the fishing fleet as a space to dry nets, and converted to a promenade during the Regency.

The garden at the southern end is dominated by Victoria Fountain *(photograph right)*, which was erected to celebrate the young Queen's twenty-seventh birthday. It stands on a ring of ancient sarsen stones, which littered the area and gave the road its name. On the West side stands Marlborough House, once the home of the Duke of Marlborough and the work of architect Robert Adam. Next door is Steine House, built for Mrs Fitzherbert, the 'secret' wife of the Prince of Wales. Now the YMCA, it contains an imitation bamboo staircase in cast iron similar to those in the Royal Pavilion.

Just beyond the Royal Pavilion on the Western side of the parade narrow streets lead into the North Laine. This group of streets was originally Brighton's market garden, but was built over between 1820-1840 with the industrialisation of the town. It is now firmly identified as Brighton's bohemian quarter, full of small independent shops, cafes and bars. Saturday morning is the best time to visit, when cars are barred from the streets to make way for bric-a-brac stalls and the tables and chairs from the cafes.

St Peter's church *(photograph above)*, standing on a green island to the north of the Old Steine, is the parish church of Brighton. It was designed by Charles Barry, the architect who went on to design the Houses of Parliament at Westminster in the same popular Gothic revival style.

THE ROYAL PAVILION ESTATE

Without a doubt the most beautiful and extraordinary palace in Europe, the Royal Pavilion is an unmissable sight. As well as the palace itself, the little estate includes gardens landscaped to architect John Nash's original design and the former stables and riding school, now home to Brighton's Museum, Dome Theatre and Corn Exchange.

The palace itself has had a chequered history, and has only recently been fully restored to Regency splendour. Whilst George IV's successors, William and Adelaide, were also regular visitors to Brighton, it was not popular with Queen Victoria, and she announced her intention to sell the Royal Pavilion in 1846. For the next two years the contents were gradually stripped out and taken to Buckingham Palace and Windsor. It seemed as though the palace would be demolished, but the people of Brighton petitioned Parliament, and the town acquired the palace as its own. The Pavilion was used for a variety of purposes in the coming years, perhaps the strangest being that of a military hospital in the First World War for injured Indian soldiers.

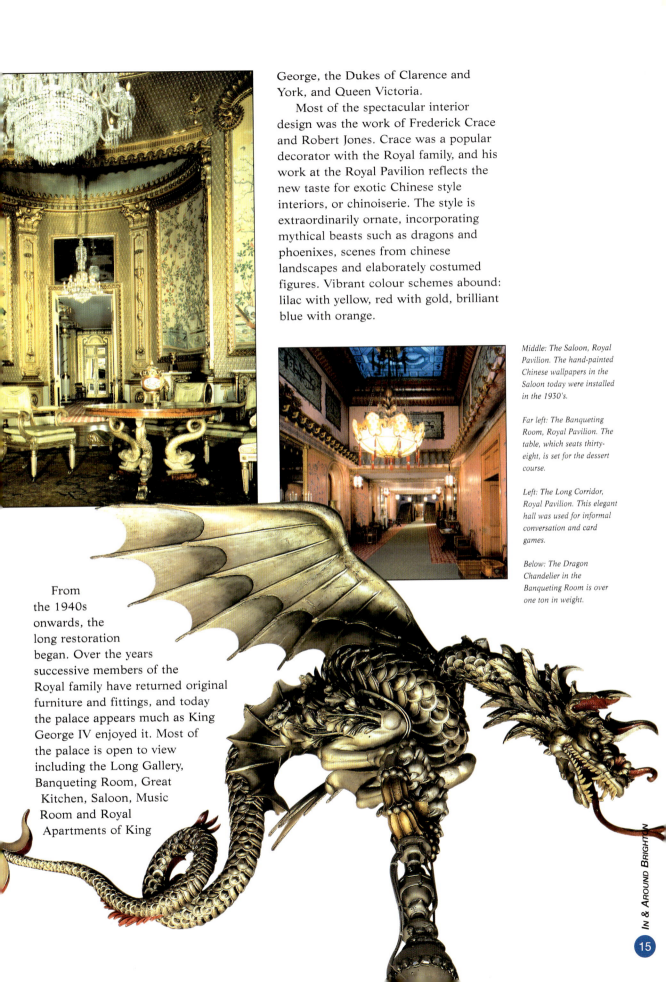

George, the Dukes of Clarence and York, and Queen Victoria.

Most of the spectacular interior design was the work of Frederick Crace and Robert Jones. Crace was a popular decorator with the Royal family, and his work at the Royal Pavilion reflects the new taste for exotic Chinese style interiors, or chinoiserie. The style is extraordinarily ornate, incorporating mythical beasts such as dragons and phoenixes, scenes from chinese landscapes and elaborately costumed figures. Vibrant colour schemes abound: lilac with yellow, red with gold, brilliant blue with orange.

From the 1940s onwards, the long restoration began. Over the years successive members of the Royal family have returned original furniture and fittings, and today the palace appears much as King George IV enjoyed it. Most of the palace is open to view including the Long Gallery, Banqueting Room, Great Kitchen, Saloon, Music Room and Royal Apartments of King

Middle: The Saloon, Royal Pavilion. The hand-painted Chinese wallpapers in the Saloon today were installed in the 1930's.

Far left: The Banqueting Room, Royal Pavilion. The table, which seats thirty-eight, is set for the dessert course.

Left: The Long Corridor, Royal Pavilion. This elegant hall was used for informal conversation and card games.

Below: The Dragon Chandelier in the Banqueting Room is over one ton in weight.

Above: The Great Kitchen from Nash's 'Views of the Royal Pavilion'. The Kitchen was superbly equipped for its day.

Right: Faience Cat by Emile Gallé, c.1880. One of a pair on display in the decorative arts gallery at the Brighton Museum & Art Gallery.

Besides the opulence, the Pavilion was noted for its innovations in modern living. Gas was used to light the building - to particularly dramatic effect in the stairways, where huge painted glass panels were lit from behind in the evening. The Prince was particularly proud of his modern kitchen, and often invited his visitors to admire the fittings within. One of these, a huge steam table in the centre,

Left: Interior of the Royal Stables, designed by Porden, from Nash's Views.

where dishes could be kept warm, enabled the chefs to serve up to thirty-six separate dishes piping hot at the same time.

The landscaped gardens around the Pavilion have only recently been restored to the picturesque layout of the 1820s. Both the gateways into the grounds are later additions. The square India Gate on the south side was donated by that country in thanks for the role the palace served during the First World War. The northern entrance, King William IV Gate, was erected in 1832. Just outside this gate is a statue of George IV by Sir Francis Chantry.

Adjacent to it, the old coach houses and stables became the Brighton Museum and Art Gallery in 1873. This fine building has a lavishly tiled Moorish entrance hall. The museum collections are particularly noted for nineteenth and early twentieth century decorative art, furniture and porcelain. There are also substantial ethnography collections, as well as fashion, local history, archaeology and musical instruments.

Next to the museum is the Dome theatre *(photograph above)*, originally The Prince of Wales's stables. The great dome is eighty feet in diameter, one of the largest in the world at the time it was completed. A long tunnel connected the Dome to the royal apartments, allowing the Prince direct, private access to his stables. The building was converted to a concert hall in 1867, and underwent refurbishment in the 1930's. The Art Deco interior is now listed. The Dome theatre is the largest of the three on New Road, and is now mainly used for concerts. It was the scene of triumph for the pop group Abba in 1974, when they won the Eurovision song contest here with 'Waterloo'.

The Corn Exchange, next door was originally the riding school, but is now used as an exhibition hall.

HOVE

The boundary between the two towns of Brighton and Hove is barely noticeable along Western Road, the main thoroughfare. A small sign high on the wall of a side street is the only indication that you have crossed the border into the Brunswick estate and Hove. Above the great seafront sweep of Adelaide Crescent is Palmeira Square, an elegant development of the mid-1800's, built on the site of the Antheum, a great domed conservatory which unfortunately collapsed when the scaffolding was taken down on opening day! Excavation at Palmeira Square revealed ancient occupation of the site, and an extraordinary bronze age solid amber cup, one of the treasures of the town, was found here. To the north of the square, a floral clock in the gardens commemorates the coronation of the present Queen in 1953. At the far end of New Church Road, the main shopping street of the town, is Hove Museum and Art Gallery (photograph below), which has a particular focus on regional crafts plus displays on the early film industry. In the grounds is an elaborately carved teak gateway, the Jaipur Gate, a gift from India in 1866.

The British Engineerium, in Nevill Road, is a former water pumping station. Now a museum of industrial history, it celebrates the achievements of the steam age. Not far away is Blatchington Mill, a traditional smock windmill, and the Foredown Tower, a converted water tower which houses a camera obscura, satellite weather station, and local centre for conservation.

OTHER PLACES OF INTEREST

The Booth Museum

The Booth Museum of Natural History lies about a mile from the town centre along Dyke Road. It was built by the eminent Victorian naturalist and collector William Booth, to house his extensive collection of birds. These are on display in their original showcases, which line the walls of the museum

Below: The Drawing Room, Preston Manor. This formal reception room reflects the style and taste of the early twentieth century.

from floor to ceiling. The collection also includes displays of skeletons, fossils, geology and the natural history of Sussex.

Patcham and Preston

These two little villages now form part of the northern suburb of Brighton. Preston Manor, *(photograph below)* an Edwardian country house, is open to the public, and vividly portrays life both above and below stairs. It was given to the town as a bequest from the Stanford family in 1925. The Stanfords at one time owned considerable areas of land in Brighton, and the fine house reflects the taste and comforts of a wealthy Edwardian family. There are good collections of furniture and porcelain, and a number of Edwardian events are held throughout the year. The gardens reveal the older history of the site, its thick flint walls probably those of the ancient Manor which was held by the Bishop of Chichester for almost five hundred years.

Close by the house, St Peter's church dates from 1250. Preston Park is Brighton's biggest park, and includes a fabulous rock garden, floodlit at night, a fine clocktower and scented gardens.

In Patcham village, there are some very fine cottages in the Square and on Church Hill, the church itself dating from the twelfth century.

Standing on the summit of the Downs above Patcham is an exotic monument, the Chattri. On this spot the Indian soldiers who had died at the Royal Pavilion hospital during the first World War were cremated. The octagonal white marble monument, like a miniature temple, was erected here in 1921 in their memory.

Brighton Marina
Plans for a marina for Brighton go back to the nineteenth century, but it was not until the 1960's that building began on the foreshore just beyond Kemp Town. The marina was the ambitious dream of a keen local yachtsman, Harry Cohen, but the plan was not universally popular. After polls were conducted in the town, two planning enquiries and debates in the Houses of Parliament, the scheme finally went ahead, and was opened in 1979 as Europe's largest marina, enclosing some 77 acres of sheltered water. Subsequent developments included the marina village, shopping squares and waterside pubs and restaurants. Access to the pontoons is restricted, although some pleasure craft do tour from the marina, and in the summertime a catamaran service takes day trippers to France.

THE SOUTH DOWNS

Bramber

An ancient settlement in the lee of the South Downs, the little village of Bramber has a substantial castle ruin *(photograph below)* on the outskirts. Built in 1070 by William de Broase, a knight of the Norman Conquest, on the site of an earlier Saxon fortification, the castle remained in use for centuries. It was finally destroyed during the English Civil War by Parliamentary troops, who also turned the adjacent church into a gunnery.

Nearby in the village centre is St Mary's, an exceedingly fine timber house built in 1470 by the Bishop of Winchester. Although it is a private house, the pretty gardens are opened for part of the summer months *(photograph below)*.

Devil's Dyke

Breathtaking views across the Weald for over thirty miles are what brings most visitors up to this blustery point. The ramparts of an Iron Age hill fort can still be seen near the car park. The deep valley below, formed as the glaciers retreated during the ice age, has an artificial appearance, giving rise to the legend that the Devil dug it through the Downs to flood the Christian churches of the Weald beyond. Below the Downs, a celebrated spring runs through the village of Fulking, and was used as a sheepwash by Downsmen from miles around - The Shepherd and Dog Inn on the corner gets its name from the practice.

Ditchling

This attractive little market town has over the years attracted more than its fair share of creative residents, including the artist Frank Brangwyn, sculptor Eric Gill and actress Dame Ellen Terry. Like so many other Downland villages, it has a beacon site on the hill above.

A little to the south is Clayton, home of two of East Sussex's most famous landmarks, the Jack and Jill windmills. Jill *(photograph right)*, a white painted post mill, is the oldest, and was originally built on Dyke Road in Brighton in 1821, moving to

Clayton thirty years later. Jack, a brick tower mill, was built alongside in 1866. Badly dilapidated this century, Jack was rescued by Universal Pictures, who restored the mill for a sequence in the Film 'The Black Windmill'.

Rottingdean

A pretty village four miles east of Brighton with a good beach. The fine village green, with a traditional pond, runs alongside The Elms, former home of Rudyard Kipling. The Kipling garden adjacent is particularly charming. Across the grass is the former home of the eminent Pre-Raphaelite, Edward Burne Jones. He is buried in the churchyard of St Margaret's *(photograph left)*, and the church holds a number of stained glass windows by him.

Facing the village green is Rottingdean Grange, a fine Georgian house with a small museum and tea gardens.

Around the corner from the church, Tudor Cottages *(photograph above)* were in fact built this century, although these picturesque little house do include some original Tudor features salvaged from old buildings. The actress Bette Davis lived here for a short time.

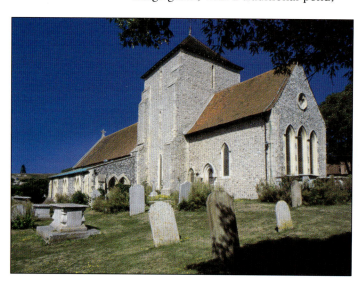

Lewes

Lewes is the County town of Sussex, despite its small size. A Saxon stronghold, it passed to a Norman knight, William de Warenne, after the conquest. The castle *(photograph right)* was first built by him in 1078. From the ramparts one can look down on the site of the Battle of Lewes, where Henry III was defeated by Simon de Montford in 1264.

During the sixteenth century, religious upheavals led to the execution of seventeen Protestant martyrs in the town. The town has remained fiercely proud of its Protestant heritage ever since, and commemorates the martyrdom every year in a spectacular parade and bonfire on November the fifth. Those born in Lewes are entitled to join one of several guilds, whose rivalry in constructing the finest floats, costumes and fires for the occasion is fierce.

There are fine medieval buildings on the town, particularly Anne of Cleeves house, formerly the property of Henry VIII's wife, and now a museum.

large flotilla of sailing boats leave Brighton Marina in an attempt to make the crossing in the fastest time.

During November, conservation week at the Royal Pavilion includes opportunities to look behind the scenes at the work of the conservators, carpenters, upholsterers and gilders who are continually at work restoring the Palace. In the first week of November, the famous veteran car rally runs from Hyde Park in London to Brighton seafront. Several hundred vehicles take part in the famous race. In December, the Burning of the Clocks *(photograph below)* on Brighton beach lights up the winter sky. Huge

SPECIAL EVENTS

Brighton's annual Festival of the Arts is second only to Edinburgh in size, and runs from the beginning of May to early June. There are a wide number of theatrical and musical events at all the town's theatres, and various art exhibitions, including an 'open house' week, where local artists and craftspeople open up their homes and studios to visitors. A spectacular parade and fireworks display on the beach are always part of the proceedings.

September sees the dramatic re-enactment of the Royal Escape, when King Charles II escaped across the sea to Fecamp in France. A

clocks are constructed of paper and wood by local schoolchildren, who parade from Pavilion Gardens to the beach before setting the clocks alight, in an old Brighton tradition whose origins are unknown. These fires are not as spectacular however as those held in Lewes on November Fifth, when the entire town, along with around forty thousand onlookers, gathers for bonfire celebrations *(photograph page 29)*. Torchlit processions of the bonfire guilds, bands, tableaux and burning tar barrel races are all part of the riotous celebrations in honour of the Protestant martyrs of Lewes.

IN & AROUND Brighton & HOVE

1. The Royal Pavilion
2. Town Hall
3. Dome Theatre
4. Brighton Museum & Art Gallery
5. St Peter's Church
6. Volk's Electric Railway
7. Brighton Sea Life Centre (Brighton Aquarium)
8. Hove Museum & Art Gallery